Original title:
Wreath of Words

Copyright © 2025 Creative Arts Management OÜ
All rights reserved.

Author: Finn Donovan
ISBN HARDBACK: 978-1-80567-012-4
ISBN PAPERBACK: 978-1-80567-092-6

A Circle of Lingering Stanzas

In a circle of thoughts, they gather,
Jokes spun like yarn, some light as a feather.
Words tumble down, a playful dance,
Each line a twirl, an unexpected chance.

With giggles and puns, they twist and sway,
Rolling like marbles, they play all day.
A chorus of chuckles, a literary spree,
In this merry ring, we're all feeling free.

The Looping Lattice of Lore

Stories ensnared in a web so tight,
Crafting tall tales, from day into night.
A pun here, a jest there, they stitch and weave,
Making folks giggle, it's hard to believe.

Round and round, the laughter spins,
Where everyone seeks to share their wins.
A loop of humor, a crafty delight,
Each quip a lantern, glowing so bright.

Serpentine Shadows of Prose

In shadows that slither like serpents at play,
The words sneak out with a twist and a sway.
Each sentence a squiggle, a wiggly line,
Dancing through pages, they sparkle and shine.

They curl and they laugh, in the night they do roam,
Like mischief-makers far from their home.
Whispering secrets that tickle the mind,
In this funny dance, good humor we find.

Interwoven Expressions of the Heart

Hearts intertwined with laughter and cheer,
Each stitch a moment, so precious and dear.
Witty remarks that flutter about,
Bringing bright smiles, banishing doubt.

Threads of good humor craft bonds so tight,
In this fabric of joy, everything feels right.
Expressions that mingle like colors in art,
A canvas of humor, straight from the heart.

The Fabric of Language

In the loom of speech, threads tangle tight,
Words dance around, what a silly sight!
Puns weave in and out, like jokes on a spree,
Who knew grammar could tickle with glee?

Syntax takes a tumble, like socks in a spin,
Adjectives fly around, let the laughter begin!
Metaphors wearing hats of various styles,
Make meaning a game with humorous miles.

Delicate Threads of Thought

In the tapestry of thought, colors clash and cheer,
Ideas popping loudly, like corn when it's near!
Giggles round the corners, thoughts twist and twine,
A jumbled mess of meanings, oh, how they shine!

Like noodles in a pot, they wiggle and squirm,
Each twist a funny moment, a jest or a term.
Creations of absurdity hang boldly on shelves,
Crafted from the humor we conjure ourselves.

Circle of Rhyme

Round and round we go, with a jig and a jiggle,
Each rhyme like a tickle, a giggle and wiggle!
A carousel of nonsense, spinning with glee,
Who knew words could dance like the leaves from a tree?

It's a rhythm of folly, a melodic delight,
Where ducks wear top hats and cats take flight.
In this playful domain, let giggles abound,
For the art of the silly knows no bounds!

Petals of Poetry

In the garden of verses, blossoms in bloom,
Each line is a petal, scoffing at gloom.
Sunshine and laughter, bees buzzing near,
This floral rebellion brings joy and good cheer!

Daisies of humor with quips that adorn,
Tickle our senses from evening to morn.
Each stanza a flower, unique and absurd,
Together they giggle, a chorus of words!

The Arc of Aesthetics

In twisted lines, the letters dance,
They prance around like kids in pants.
With giggles wrapped in every phrase,
They turn the mundane into a maze.

A sonnet shaped like a funny hat,
With puns that wiggle, where's the cat?
Each verse a joke with winks and cheers,
As prose takes flight on silly tears.

Sentiments in Bloom

Thoughts blossom out like daisies wild,
And every rhyme is just a child.
With laughter faint and blooms so bright,
They tickle noses, a pure delight.

Each petal unfurls a tale so neat,
With humor that dances on light feet.
Quotes swirling like bees in glee,
Who knew a stanza could be so free?

The Union of Uproar

In chaos, they gather, a merry crew,
With pranks and puns that make you go 'whoo!'
Each line a jester in court of rhyme,
Spinning tales that tickle, all in good time.

They shout and frolic, creating a mess,
In the garden of giggles, they feel so blessed.
Words clash and collide, like pies in the sky,
Creating a ruckus, oh me, oh my!

Whispers in the Weave

Silk threads of laughter entwined with flair,
In whispers that glide through the sunlit air.
Jokes stitched slowly in a fabric bright,
That shimmer and shimmer in the gentle light.

Each stitch a chuckle, each knot a grin,
With patterns of joy knitted deep within.
In this tapestry of glee, we find,
That humor's the craft that binds all mankind.

Streams of Story

In a land where tales run wild,
A dragon danced, a knight just smiled.
The castles were made of candy sweet,
With gummy bears stuck to their feet.

A fish wore glasses, reading a book,
While the cat in boots gave a sly look.
The moon played hide and seek with the sun,
Oh, what a world, where laughter's spun!

The trees hummed tunes, as squirrels took flight,
Playing chess with the stars each night.
A talking pie shared jokes with a cake,
And ice cream cones began to shake.

So gather your tales, let laughter bloom,
In this zany world, there's always room.
For stories that tickle and make us cheer,
In these streams of story, fun's always near!

Flows of Fancy

Imagine a world of jellybeans,
Where everyone wears candy-coated jeans.
A giraffe plays hopscotch on a cloud,
And the marshmallow people sing out loud.

The sun's a chef with a frying pan bright,
Cooking up dreams in the dead of night.
The rivers flow with chocolate delight,
As frogs serenade the starry night.

Dancing lollipops twirl 'round the trees,
While gumdrops giggle in the breeze.
The cake is a castle, not made of stone,
Where giggly knights call it home, all alone.

In this flow of fancy, joy reigns supreme,
Where we savor each whimsy and every dream.
So take a step into this land of play,
Where laughter and joy lead the way!

A Cascade of Connections

In a realm where socks have a chat,
And cats are busy with a daily spat.
A parrot plays chess with a wise old fox,
As they sit by the river made of frocks!

Jellyfish don hats, looking quite grand,
While umbrellas tango on the soft sand.
Clouds wear pajamas, oh what a sight,
As colors dance in the warm daylight.

A raccoon juggles fruit with flair,
And giggling gnomes jump everywhere.
Cupcakes hold court with a raspberry crown,
Spinning tales in a whimsical town.

In this cascade of laughter, let's weave,
Together in joy, it's hard to believe!
With every giggle, a bond will grow,
In this merry realm, where fun's on show!

Resonance in Rhymes

In a land where puns run wild,
Jokes are crafted, quite beguiled.
With giggles floating through the air,
Laughter dances everywhere.

A spoonerism here, a twist there,
Makes even the grumpiest declare.
Words play tag in silly ways,
They prance around like kids at play.

Quips and quotes, a playful chase,
With laughter plastered on each face.
Jokesters gather, brew their schemes,
Lively banter fills the beams.

So let us toast to crafty puns,
Where merriment just never shuns.
In this realm of rhythmic cheer,
Every word feels like a beer.

The Emblem of Essence

A comic strip of thoughts unfurls,
Where every phrase makes laughter twirl.
A giggle here, a chuckle there,
In this jesting, silly air.

Punchlines race like runners swift,
Each clever quip, a cherished gift.
In jest, the world seems light and bright,
As humor dances day and night.

With witticisms thick as glue,
They take us where the chuckles grew.
A punchy tale, a twist of fate,
In this humor-filled, joyous state.

So gather 'round and have a share,
In this emblem of laughter rare.
For in each quirk and playful jest,
Lives the spirit of life at its best.

A Cascade of Creativity

In the garden of quirky thoughts,
We plant the seeds of funny plots.
A drizzle of whimsy, a sprinkle of cheer,
A playful spirit draws us near.

With each bright bloom, a jest will rise,
From rainy jokes to sunny sighs.
We dance with words like butterflies,
Creativity's jaunt never dies.

A tapestry woven of humor rich,
With threads of laughter, a perfect stitch.
Each pun, a petal, soft and light,
A splash of joy, a spark of delight.

So let us frolic in this space,
With plenty of joy, and a little grace.
In this cascade where giggles flow,
We celebrate all the fun we know.

Language's Labyrinth

Down the winding trails we roam,
In this maze, we find our home.
Words like breadcrumbs lead the way,
Through funny turns, where jesters play.

Each corner hides a pun or rhyme,
In this wacky realm, lost in time.
With riddles waiting to unveil,
In this delightful, silly trail.

Banter echoes off each wall,
As laughter bounces, we enthrall.
Every turn brings a new surprise,
In this labyrinth with warm, bright eyes.

So join the quest, let laughter guide,
Through witty paths we choose with pride.
In this playful maze of glee,
Words twist and twirl, so merrily.

Cadence of the Celestial Scribe

In the cosmos where quills take flight,
Stars tickle pages, oh what a sight!
Comets write sonnets in sparkling streams,
While planets play tag in whimsical dreams.

Galaxies giggle as they spin and twirl,
Black holes laugh loud, give time a whirl!
The moon winks softly, tossing out rhymes,
In this stellar theater that juggles the times.

Supernovae burst in comedic flair,
While asteroids dance, in perpetual air.
With laughter they ink, in galaxies wide,
A tale of the heavens with humor inside.

Each line drips stardust, a chuckle or two,
For even the cosmos knows how to stew!
In this cadence of scribes, bright and bizarre,
The universe chuckles, a cosmic bazaar.

Garland of Gamboling Verses

Poets pretend to be wise, oh so grand,
While scribbling nonsense with a shaky hand.
They slip on the ink, fall flat on their face,
Claiming it's art, a ridiculous race.

The lines twist like pretzels, they bend and they break,
Each word a confetti, for laughter's own sake.
Sunshine giggles, rainbows pop up,
As verses pirouette like a clumsy pup.

Limericks tumble, rolling on the floor,
Chasing after jests like a playful core.
In this garland of giggles, the fun never stops,
As light-hearted verses perform comic hops.

Oh poets, you jesters, your quips fly high,
With punchlines that soar and tickle the sky.
Crafting a world where laughter's the law,
In this merry dance, they create quite the awe.

The Binding of Lyrical Dreams

In a book where the pages are giggles and glee,
Words bind together in hilarious spree.
Dreams dance on paper, in pajamas they play,
Chasing the sunset, as night steals the day.

Each line sends a tickle right down to your toes,
While rhymes wear sombreros, and everybody knows.
The ink spills some secrets, nonsensical jest,
As poets chuckle, they're simply the best!

With bookmarks of laughter, they navigate aisles,
In libraries dressed up with whimsical smiles.
The binding is sturdy, with sass and some cheer,
As lyrical dreams bring the giggles near.

So come stretch your mind and your heart to the max,
As stories unfold with delightful little cracks.
The world's a stage, and oh, what a scene,
In the realm of the funny and the wildly obscene!

Verses Woven in Twilight

Under twinkling stars, the ink takes a stand,
Witty lines wander in a whimsical band.
Night wraps its arms, with a laugh like a friend,
As shadows recount tales that seem never to end.

Giggles rise up from the depths of the dark,
Whispering secrets, igniting a spark.
The moon dons a grin, with a cheeky delight,
In this tapestry spun from the hours of night.

Jokes hang like lanterns, they flicker and sway,
As verses tumble down like leaves in a ballet.
You can't help but chuckle, the humor is grand,
In twilight's embrace, where jesters expand.

So dance on the lines, let your laughter run wild,
With each woven verse, find your inner child.
In this twilight realm, with your heart set alight,
The whispers of laughter weave dreams through the night.

Emotions Embroidered

In the closet of my mind, a colorful thread,
Stitching jumbles of laughter, where joy's often fed.
A button of worries, a patch of delight,
My quilt of emotions keeps me warm at night.

I once sewed confusion with a needle of fate,
A thimble of chaos, oh, isn't it great?
The fabric of feelings, so rich and absurd,
My tailor's a jester; my life is a word.

The Threads of Time

Time's a funky fabric, odd patterns it weaves,
Ribbons of moments, like bright falling leaves.
Tangled in laughter, I trip on the past,
Each stitch a reminder, oh, how time flies fast.

I added some colors, borrowed from the sun,
Knots of good memories, sticking like gum.
My timeline's a mess, but fun is the goal,
With threads of absurdity, I craft my whole soul.

Fractal Fragments

In a realm of odd shapes, my mind likes to roam,
Fractal funniness, it feels like a home.
Bits of nonsense, like a patchwork quilt,
Jokes in the seams, with humor they've built.

More faces than fabric, I smile with glee,
Each slice of hilarity is part of me.
Puzzle pieces jiving, all jumbled and bright,
A tapestry of laughter that feels just right.

The Bouquet of Ideas

A bouquet of thoughts, all tangled and spry,
With petals of giggles that float and fly.
Stemmed in concepts, some wobbly and wild,
A floral explosion, oh, ain't life beguiled?

Chasing the bees with quips that collide,
Mixing up metaphors, they laugh and they glide.
Each bloom is a whimsy, a garden of dreams,
Growing from silliness, or so it seems.

The Edges of Expression

In a land where giggles grow,
Words take a stroll, putting on a show.
They dance and twirl, so bold and bright,
Making every dull moment a delight.

Puns fly like butterflies in the air,
Tickling our thoughts, without a care.
Jokes bounce around like a rubber ball,
In this carnival of chatter, we have a ball.

Whispers of whimsy tickle the ear,
As laughter and smiles draw ever near.
Every phrase is a silly surprise,
In the kingdom of quirks, joy surely lies.

The Charm of Chorus

Gather 'round for a jolly verse,
Where comedy blooms and we all rehearse.
Each line sings out, like a friendly bird,
In a playful concert of laughter, absurd.

With a flick of the tongue and a wink of the eye,
Our words take flight, soaring up high.
Choruses echo, tickling the soul,
In this raucous rendering, we lose control.

Rhythms of joy drum a cheerful beat,
Making even the grumpiest wiggle their feet.
In this delightful blend of wit and glee,
Every chuckle is a note in the spree.

Patterned Reflections

In a mirror of mayhem, we gleam and glare,
Collecting our chuckles like splashes of flair.
Reflections of folly, all shapes and sizes,
Wrap us in giggles full of surprises.

Each jest paints a canvas, colorful and bright,
A tapestry of humor, a wondrous sight.
We dance with the words, in a playful embrace,
Every line, a new twist in this funny space.

Laughter spirals, a carousel ride,
In the circles of jest, our worries subside.
In patterns of humor, we find our place,
Where nonsense and joy keep up the pace.

A Ring of Revelation

In circles of chatter, wisdom goes round,
Mysteries unravel, where laughter is found.
Each chuckle a riddle, each giggle a clue,
In this playful loop, bright insights accrue.

A tickle of truth in a flurry of fun,
As punchlines emerge, our worries are done.
Around we go, like a merry-go-round,
Finding light in the quirks that abound.

With each jovial twist, new thoughts ignite,
In this ring of revelation, everything's bright.
So join the parade, let's dance and declare,
With humor as our guide, we're free as the air.

A Tapestry of Whispered Lines

In a garden of giggles, I weave my tale,
With puns that frolic like a chubby whale.
Every giggle blooms in the chatter's breeze,
Words can tickle, put hearts at ease.

A droll parade of phrases on the run,
Making our senses dance, oh what fun!
Like a jester juggling words on a line,
Here's a riddle for you: Does it rhyme or shine?

Slinky sentences spiraling with glee,
Chasing down metaphors like they're lost at sea.
Watch as the whispers take shape and spin,
Laughter is the craft, let the word games begin!

So come grab a stitch from my silly loom,
With every quip, it lights up the room.
Let's weave together, no need for a guide,
In this tapestry where humor resides.

The Circling Dance of Language

Words like waltzers in a comical spree,
Twist and turn, just like you and me.
Each giggle a step, each snicker a dash,
Together we tango, then burst out in a crash!

A boisterous ballet in the theatre of jest,
With each zany line, we give laughter a test.
We shuffle and slide through metaphoric shoes,
Where every slip-up just brings us more muse.

Can you hear the chuckles? They're following suit,
A chorus of joy, isn't that cute?
We leap to the rhythm of blissful delight,
In this dance of phrases, everything feels right.

So grab my hand, let's swirl and twirl,
Spin through the words, give the world a whirl.
In this language dance, your smile's the prize,
Let's wrap up the evening with playful goodbyes.

Enchanted Loops of Expression

Around the corner, with a wink and a grin,
Words loop like a rollercoaster, let's begin!
In a carnival of phrases, we laugh till we cry,
Jumping through laughter, we're soaring high.

Like a yo-yo of thoughts, I toss and I spin,
Each bounce a chuckle, let the fun begin!
With whimsical tangents and puns on display,
This merry-go-round of humor's here to stay.

Watch the ribbons of banter take flight in the air,
With each rising quip, we conquer despair.
We'll loop through the stories with joyful cheer,
In this magic of words, there's nothing to fear.

Our minds are the playground, so come take a ride,
With playful confessions that cannot hide.
These enchanted loops will twirl us around,
In the land of expression, hilarity's found.

Fragments of Fabled Sentences

Once upon a giggle in a story untold,
Phrases scatter like marbles, all shiny and bold.
There's whimsy in words when they tumble and roll,
Crafting fragments of nonsense, that's the goal!

In a pot full of puns, we stir up the stew,
Tasting each joke, oh, how they construe!
Metaphoric mash-ups with a sprinkle of glee,
These fabled sentences are funny as can be.

With a flick of my quill, I conjure a laugh,
Each fragment a chuckle instead of a gaffe.
They bounce on the page, like kids on the run,
In this realm of the silly, we've only begun!

So gather your words, let's mix and blend,
We'll spin tales of laughter that never will end.
From fragments to fables, let our voices ignite,
In this comedic chaos, everything's bright!

Echoes in the Garden of Verse

In the garden where giggles grow,
Each line sprouts laughter, don't you know?
Puns and rhymes dance with glee,
As bees buzz tunes, oh so free.

Jokes bloom bright 'neath sunny skies,
Silly thoughts wear clever ties.
Whispers tickle lilac blooms,
Words sway like a chorus of looms.

With every step, a chuckle waits,
Scribbled notes on garden gates.
Sprinkled humor, a playful breeze,
In this patch where whimsy agrees.

So come, dear friend, enjoy the show,
Let laughter's petals fall like snow.
In this realm where words collide,
Fun and joy are multiplied!

Threads of Thought Entwined

In the fabric of words, we stitch,
Each thought a thread, quite the niche.
Some are frayed, others quite bold,
Tales of folly, yet to be told.

Knots of nonsense twist and turn,
Fabrics where wild ideas yearn.
Laughter weaves through every seam,
Creating a tapestry of dream.

With each tug, a giggle springs,
Ideas take flight on silly wings.
Embroidered with joy, a fun design,
Crafting humor, oh so fine!

So gather round this playful loom,
Where thoughts entwine and laughter blooms.
Craft your own thread, add a dash,
In this joyous weave, take a splash!

Blossoms of Rhyme and Reason

In a field where rhymes abound,
Silly thoughts are tightly wound.
Every petal sings a tune,
Lively verses chase the moon.

Logic bends, then breaks a few,
As flowers giggle in the dew.
Petals tickle, laughter spreads,
In this patch where joy misled.

Words bloom bright, with shades of fun,
Every line a little pun.
Reason waves with a cheeky grin,
In this garden, all can win!

Dance amidst this riotous scene,
Where laughter reigns and hearts stay keen.
With blossoms full of rhyme's delight,
Your spirit dances, soaring light!

Petals of Poetic Reflection

In a mirror made of words so bright,
Reflections twist in pure delight.
Petals fall like chuckles sweet,
Each line a laugh, a warm heartbeat.

Glimmers flash from sentences spun,
Tales unfold with silly fun.
Squirrels slip on poetic slips,
Through puddles of words, their laughter drips.

Refracted joy through polished phrases,
Dancing light in comedic mazes.
Every verse a funny glance,
Inviting all to join the dance!

So peek inside this whimsical frame,
Find your own silly name to claim.
In the garden of giggles, take your stand,
Where verses beckon, hand in hand!

A Cycle of Rhythmic Revelations

In a land where jokes take flight,
Puns play tag in the warm sunlight.
Senile squirrels paint the trees,
While giggling flowers sway in the breeze.

Chickens dance in polka dots,
Grasshoppers strum on their fiddling spots.
With each chuckle, the world spins round,
And laughter echoes, a joyous sound.

In this merry-go-round of glee,
Every bird sings, 'Come play with me!'
A circus of giggles, a festival so bright,
We all take part in this comical sight.

Weaving the Fabric of Narrative

Threads of whimsy weave so tight,
Fabric of tales in the dead of night.
A cat in a hat wears boots of gold,
While knitting grand tales never told.

Ovens bake stories with jam and cream,
As toasters pop up with giggling steam.
Tangled yarns dance in playful jest,
In this world of fun, they find their rest.

Rainbow spiders spin tales that twirl,
While cookies and brownies together unfurl.
In the workshop of dreams, all's delight,
Every patch is stitched with laughter's light.

The Circle of Lingering Inspirations

Round and round, the circle spins,
Where lemon cats dance on jelly fins.
A hula hoop sings a jaunty tune,
While clowns juggle under a disco moon.

Prosciutto ghosts play hide and seek,
While bearded crabs discuss their peak.
In this merry hubbub of cheer,
Each passing joke whispers, 'Come near!'

Dance partners are pies, oh what a sight!
As we laugh and twirl under twinkling light.
In this circle of joy, no frowns allowed,
We sway and giggle, oh so proud.

Spirals of Silenced Whispers

Whispers in spirals glide with grace,
Balloons float high in a pink embrace.
The bananas wear bow ties, oh what fun,
While shy beetles dance under the sun.

Cactus serenades the sleepy moon,
As jellybeans waltz to a silly tune.
Giggling muffins, oh what a sight,
Spinning spirals in laughter's delight.

In this wild world of quirk and flair,
Silenced whispers buzz in the air.
We float and twirl, no cares in sight,
In spirals of fun, our hearts take flight.

Binding Threads of Introspection

In the attic of thought, lost socks prevail,
They dance in the shadows, telling their tale.
Each weave of a memory, a slip and a slide,
A jumble of dreams, where the silly ones hide.

With every odd knot, wisdom finds its way,
Tangles of laughter both night and the day.
Spin me a yarn that will tickle the brain,
And keep me from falling down humor's fast lane.

A needle of jest and a thread made of fun,
Stitching together what should never be done.
The fabric of folly is vivid and bright,
So let's craft a quilt under giggles tonight.

In the patchwork of life, let's not take a pause,
For folly's the thread that gives laughter its cause.
So gather your yarns, let's make something grand,
With threads of introspection, let silliness stand.

Ephemeral Loops in the Mind's Eye.

Round and round we go in this whirlwind of cheer,
   Chasing after thoughts that just vanish in air.
   Like bubbles of joy that pop with a laugh,
     Each memory danced in a humorous half.

In this carousel ride, the ducks quack aloud,
   While sheep count laughter instead of a crowd.
   The loops we create, never meant to resolve,
     But twist into giggles that we can't absolve.

Whimsical thoughts are the best kind of glue,
   Holding tight to our minds, making us feel new.
   So ride on this merry-go-round with delight,
     And let the ephemeral take wing in the night.

Each spin of the loop is a playful embrace,
   Where serious thoughts just can't find their place.
   With humor as guide, what a sight we'll behold,
     In the fleeting delight, we discover pure gold.

A Crown of Verses

In a kingdom of giggles where puns rule the day,
I wear a crown made of rhymes in disarray.
With a scepter of wisecracks and jests on my mind,
I reign over laughter, the best kind I find.

Jesters and jesting intertwine with my reign,
Celebrating the silly, it's my silly domain.
With each quirky quatrain and humorous note,
I march through the halls with a grin on my coat.

The whispers of wordplay float high in the air,
As I dance with the tales of what comical flair.
My crown of confusion is absurd but so bright,
In this kingdom of laughter, I'm queen of the night.

The festival of folly, the court full of cheer,
With every sweet verse, I hold dear and near.
So let's toast to the fun that our words can bestow,
In this crown of verses, hilarity will flow.

Echoes in the Garden

In a garden of giggles, where shadows sing loud,
The flowers are chuckling, all vibrant and proud.
The daisies are snickering, the roses all beam,
As humor takes root in this whimsical dream.

With echoes of laughter that bounce off the trees,
The butterflies flutter on the teasing breeze.
They whisper sweet jokes to the petals ahead,
While the sun chuckles softly as flowers are fed.

Each bloom wears a smile, a story to tell,
Of humorous moments in which we all dwell.
In this garden of mirth, where nonsense does flourish,
Every twinkle of wit makes the audience nourish.

So let us partake in this echoing fun,
With blossoms of laughter 'til day is all done.
In the garden, we gather, with memories so dear,
And bloom with a chuckle, sharing joy far and near.

The Spiral of Sentiments

In a land where giggles grow,
Riddles dance with a wiggly flow.
Thoughts twist, turn, and slide,
A merry-go-round of phrases abide.

Whimsical whispers fill the air,
Jokes and jests everywhere to share.
Puns flutter like butterflies bright,
Tickling minds with pure delight.

Silly hats with words we wear,
Each one winking, full of flair.
Laughter blooms in every nook,
As we scribble our funny book.

So grab a line, don't be shy,
Let your silliness graze the sky.
In this spiral of jolly cheer,
We find our joy, crystal clear.

Threads of Inspiration

With threads of humor, we will sew,
A tapestry where giggles flow.
Laughter gaps where thoughts entwine,
Knitting joy, a sight divine.

Each stitch a chuckle, each knot a grin,
We sparkle brighter than we've ever been.
Inspiration's a silly affair,
With ideas bouncing here and there.

We weave our tales with bouncy yarn,
Creating smiles that never scorn.
Ideas frolic, like kittens play,
Spinning tales in a goofy way.

So grab your thread, come join the fun,
Together we shine like the sun.
In a world sewn tight with cheer,
Our laughter echoes far and near.

The Interlace of Ideals

In a jumble of thoughts so spry,
Where piano keys giggle and sigh.
We weave our dreams in knots of bright,
Illuminating the silliness of night.

Each idea prances, skips, and hops,
Creating a patchwork that never stops.
Exuberant minds twirl and glide,
In this joyful dance, we take pride.

Frivolous fancies intertwine,
Spirits rise like bubbling wine.
Create a notion, let it fly,
With whimsy wrapped in a sparkling tie.

So why not giggle, why not play?
Let's interlace our quirks today.
In this twisted realm of delight,
Our ideals shine, truly bright.

Songs from the Heart

Oh let us sing of silly things,
Where laughter buzzes and joy springs.
Tunes of whimsy lift the mood,
A playlist brightens every brood.

With chirpy lyrics that dance and tease,
Funny tales, a whimsical breeze.
In every chorus, a giggle hides,
Among the rhythm, pure joy abides.

So let's compose a joyful tune,
Under the sun, beneath the moon.
Each note a tickle, every beat a cheer,
Creating songs we hold so dear.

With laughter woven in our hearts,
Together we craft our funny arts.
In this melody of funny delight,
We revel in joy, oh what a sight!

The Lattice of Language

In a garden of phrases, they twine,
Words dancing like bees on the vine.
With metaphors buzzing around,
A pun's laughter, so joyfully found.

Syntax plays hopscotch all day,
In this linguistic game, we sway.
A simile slides on a pun,
And all the while, we just have fun.

Each phrase is a stitch in the quilt,
Of vibrant ideas, whimsically built.
Colloquialisms tickle the ear,
With a chuckle and grin, we draw near.

So grab a word, let it roll,
Like a playful dog on a stroll.
In this fabric where humor breeds,
Language is laughter, indeed it leads.

Notes of Nuance

In a symphony of silly sounds,
Witty waves bounce all around.
Notes of nuance dance in glee,
Harmonizing with a cup of tea.

A quip here, a pun there,
Jokes float softly in the air.
With every twist of a tongue,
A chuckle awaits if you're young.

Like a cat with nine lives at play,
Each statement pounces, delights in sway.
Throw in some sarcasm for spice,
Life's a joke, just roll the dice.

So let's compose this joyful tune,
Under the light of a laughing moon.
Words play tag in the bright sunlight,
Crafting fun from morning till night.

A Circle of Craft

In the roundabout of quirky rhyme,
Crafting chaos, passing time.
A circle spins with playful grace,
Each line is a jester, a smiling face.

We weave in puns, those crafty knots,
In language's art, we tie our thoughts.
Like juggling clowns on a stormy night,
Every word is a spark, pure delight.

With a twist and a turn, it takes flight,
The magic of humor, shining bright.
In this circle, we dance and sway,
Finding joy in what we say.

So bring your whimsy, round we go,
In the craftsmanship of laughter's flow.
Each phrase we paint with silly hues,
In this merry craft, we can't lose.

The Odyssey of Expression

On a ship of words, we sail today,
Through waves of laughter, come what may.
Each expression a treasure, we'd find,
Rich with humor, playful and blind.

In the storm of stanzas, we'll ride,
With metaphors as our trustworthy guide.
Navigate puns like stars in the night,
Finding joy in this humorous flight.

Adventures slip from our tongues,
Like tropical fruit, sweet and young.
In this epic, we'll boldly speak,
With jokes so lively, they'll make us peak.

At the end of the journey, we'll cheer,
For the tales spun in laughter near.
In the vast sea of playful command,
Expression's the ship, and humor's our land.

Enchanted Scripts

A quill danced wildly on the page,
It scribbled nonsense, a merry rage.
Sentences tumbled, tripping in glee,
Words in a tangle, oh what a spree!

The ink did giggle, a splatter of fun,
As the letters sprinted, one by one.
A comma slipped, and a period rolled,
In the story's chaos, new jokes unfold.

Adjectives bounced, like they just won a game,
Verbs swung by, shouting out names.
The paragraphs danced, in a joyous whirl,
Creating a ruckus, with each playful twirl.

In this enchanted land where laughter stays,
Each word is chuckling in silly ways.
So read these scripts with a silly grin,
Join the merriment, let the giggles begin!

Nature's Narratives

In the forest's heart, squirrels play tag,
A cheeky raccoon, wearing a rag.
Trees gossip softly with swaying leaves,
While the flowers wink, oh how nature believes!

A bumblebee buzzed, with a hat made of fluff,
It said, "Too sweet! Can't get enough!"
The sunbeams chuckled as they peeked through,
Painting the world in a bright, golden hue.

Frogs croaked jokes from their lily pad throne,
While fish splashed water, laughing alone.
The sky rolled its eyes in a cloud-covered way,
Bringing rainbows out for a colorful play.

Nature's stories bloom with silly delight,
Where critters and colors dance day and night.
Join the fun in this jocular scene,
And laugh with the flowers, oh what a dream!

Tales in a Tangle

Once in a land where stories collide,
A cat wore a cape, and took silly strides.
He chased after tales, with a laugh and a purr,
While a mouse in glasses scribbled a blur.

Words tangled up like spaghetti on plates,
Sentences snickered, they shared all their mates.
A dragon in flip-flops, so quirky and bold,
Swapped stories with owls, oh the laughter they told!

In a library, where bookworms do roam,
Each page turned giggled, "This is our home!"
Tales spun together in a whimsical dance,
Tickling the minds that dared to take the chance.

So gather your stories, let the fun commence,
In this tangled realm, every word's intense.
With laughter and joy in every page curled,
These tales will tickle and brighten your world!

Stories Woven Gently

In a cozy nook, stories sweetly collide,
A bear in pajamas happily sighed.
With tea in his paws and a book on his knee,
He read of adventures, oh so carefree!

The tales wove knots like yarn from a cat,
A puzzled dog pondered, "What's all this at?"
Characters jumbled, but joy was the key,
Their stories entwined, as funny as can be.

A fox in a tutu danced to a tune,
While a hedgehog crooned to the silvery moon.
The pages flipped over, like somersaults grand,
With giggles and chuckles, hand in hand.

So sip your tea and dive in with a grin,
To stories woven where laughter begins!
In this gentle realm of whimsy and rhyme,
Every word a smile, every giggle a chime!

Colors of Communication

In a world where colors clash,
Red says stop, green makes a dash.
Yellow giggles, blue feels blue,
Purple whispers, "I'm not through!"

Orange dances, pink gives a twirl,
While brown just sits, a sleepy swirl.
Words in shades, a vibrant scene,
Talking loud, but oh so lean!

Each hue has tales it longs to share,
A rainbow's debate, if you dare.
Chitchat's messy, paint it bright,
A canvas of chat from morning till night!

So grab a brush, make voices loud,
With a splash of fun, draw your crowd.
In this spectrum where all can play,
The colors of chat brighten the day!

A Forest of Fables

In a forest dense with tales of cheer,
Trees gossip softly, lend an ear.
Squirrels chatter, birds take flight,
Each critter has a story that's just right.

The old oak chuckles, its roots run deep,
The pine winks, while others creep.
Breezes carry whispers, tales do entwine,
Under the canopy, all's just fine.

A fox sneezes, tales everyday,
The rabbits giggle, hop away.
Every leaf holds a tale, not a bore,
A comic romp through nature's door!

So wander inside this whimsy wild,
Where every tree has a story, beguiled.
A forest of fables, laughter galore,
Nature's punchline, always wanting more!

The Symphony of Soliloquies

In a theater where solos play,
Each echo has something to say.
A mime mumbles, the crowd looks sly,
While shadows sing in the darkened sky.

A speechless tale, a laugh or two,
As the curtains rise, who knows what's new?
With every pause, a twist or spin,
The orchestra warms, let the fun begin!

The spotlight shines on sass and glee,
A solo act with a dash of spree.
Each voice a note in wild array,
The symphony plays, "Come laugh and stay!"

So take a seat, indulge in the show,
With giggles and chuckles, let laughter flow.
A performance of fun, what a delight!
In this comedic concert, all feels right!

Treasures of Transcription

On pages scattered, a treasure trove,
Words in quirk, like a playful grove.
Jumbled jots, a scribble spree,
An artistic mess that sets thoughts free.

With sticky notes waving, a parade of quirks,
Each line a laugh, where humor lurks.
The pen dances wildly, strokes full of glee,
Creating a world that's silly, you see!

Captured moments, like fireflies caught,
In a jar of doodles, my mind's hot pot.
A snapshot of smiles, each word a friend,
In this transcription, the fun won't end!

So pen your own treasure, let it unfold,
In the silly script, let your heart be bold.
Every line a giggle, every phrase a cheer,
In this madness of words, let laughter steer!

Spirits of Syntax

In the garden of phrases, they prance,
With commas and colons, they twirl and dance.
Riddles float like bubbles, full of cheer,
While verbs play hopscotch, it's quite the spectacle here.

Conjunctions are giggling, sharing their tales,
Adjectives arm-wrestle, creating grand scales.
Puns take the stage, with wigs and a flair,
As nouns juggle laugh lines, floating through air.

Every exclamation jumps up with delight,
As metaphors kick off their shoes for the night.
The syntax spins stories, wild in their flight,
Where laughter sprouts roots in the soft, starry light.

In this punctuation party, no one feels small,
Each sentence a dancer, invited to ball.
So join in the fun, let your grammar unfold,
With spirits of syntax, let joy be retold.

The Intertwined Journey

Words set off traveling, packed with a grin,
Adverbs are the guides, ensuring we win.
On a road of reflections, they gather and sway,
As nouns take a selfie, brightening the day.

Metaphors climb mountains, so bold and so free,
While similes sip tea, under the old tree.
They hitch a ride on rhyme, not a care in the world,
As puns throw confetti, laughter unfurled.

In the land of expressions, where gags never die,
A syntax parade marches, with banners held high.
Witty repartees weave through the air like fine lace,
As humor and wisdom take turns in the race.

With each playful step, a new story pops up,
They'll laugh at the chaos, then share with a cup.
The journey is endless, their passion grows more,
In this whacky adventure, there's always much more.

The Chorus of Chosen Words

In the concert of language, a melody plays,
Puns strike a chord, in the sun's shining rays.
Vowels take center stage, with rhythms so bright,
As consonants chip in, adding to the light.

Verses all gather, a crowd of delight,
To sing silly ballads, from morning to night.
An ellipsis does cartwheels, with flair and with grace,
While metaphors serenade in a warm, cozy space.

Each stanza a note, in this catchy refrain,
Quirky and cheerful, like sunshine through rain.
As idioms rise up, with a wink and a twist,
The audience chuckles, for none can resist.

Together they harmonize, laughter the key,
Unruly but lovely, oh what a spree!
In the chorus of choices, find joy that won't cease,
Where funny and clever harmoniously meet.

Cascade of Cognition

Thoughts tumble like water, cascading with glee,
Each splash is a pun that tickles the knee.
Ideas flow freely, like rivers they roam,
While questions float by, inviting you home.

With logic as stepping stones, vibrant and bright,
Each hypothesis hops, bringing thoughts to light.
Synonyms slide down, in a slippery race,
As adjectives spiral, each finding its place.

In this cognitive wonder, connect and explore,
With laughter as current, who could ask for more?
Imaginations soar, diving deep from the shore,
As wisdom and whimsy unlock every door.

So ride on this stream, let the banter unfurl,
In the cascade of insight, let laughter swirl.
For in every small ripple, a giggle will bloom,
Where cognition collides and brightens the room.

Cadence in the Blooming Void

In the garden of nonsense, we dance with glee,
Petals of laughter, tickled by the bees.
Blossoms of whimsy, in every zone,
Giggles and guffaws, the flowers have grown.

As we plant our puns, the soil does chuckle,
Each seed a punchline, a verbal shuffle.
With roots intertwined, in chaos we play,
A comedy plot in the light of day.

Silly daffodils poke, saying 'Look at me!'
While roses throw shade like a comedian's spree.
The daisies crack up, rolling on the ground,
In this blooming void, where laughter is found.

So let's tiptoe through jokes, on petals we glide,
In a world of absurdity, joy we can't hide.
Amidst all the blossoms, let folly take flight,
As we twirl through the garden, what a silly sight!

Scrolls of Unspoken Dreams

In a library of giggles, where silence is loud,
Bookmarks are secrets, each page in a shroud.
Unraveled tales whisper on paper so thin,
As dreams write their stories with a mischievous grin.

A scroll unfurls, and who should appear?
A jester, a riddle, with jokes to endear.
Between every word lies a chuckle or two,
As sentences tumble, they dance and they skew.

The ink runs wild, as the puns take their stance,
Each letter a partner, we waltz in a trance.
In these unspoken dreams, where giggles reside,
A banquet of nonsense, let laughter preside.

With every new chapter, a snicker or sigh,
These scrolls of delight, oh they surely fly high!
So open a page, let the chuckles unfold,
In the library of laughs, let our stories be told.

The Embrace of Elusive Metaphors

In a land of strange riddles, where meanings play hide,
Metaphors hug tightly, with nonsense as guide.
A fish holds a pencil, writing tales in the air,
While the clouds sip on soda, without any care.

Jumping through adjectives, a trampoline dreams,
Swirling in similes, bursting at the seams.
The sun wears a top hat, quite dapper and bright,
As shadows do tango, oh what a delight!

With roots tangled up in hilarious glee,
Every phrase is a puzzle, talking nonsense to me.
Metaphors giggle, sneaking a peek,
In this embrace of humor, it's laughter we seek.

So let's frolic through phrases that twist and that turn,
In this playground of words, where laughter we earn.
For the play of the language, oh what a delight,
In the embrace of the silly, we dance into night!

A Mosaic of Dreamt Connections

Bits of thoughts scattered like glittering stars,
Each one a connection, from Venus to Mars.
In this mosaic bright, where giggles entwine,
We stitch up the moments, like fabric divine.

A patchwork of puns sewn with threads of light,
Bringing together, the silly and bright.
In corners of whimsy, where ideas collide,
We drape our connections in laughter and pride.

With buttons of joy, on this quilt we create,
Each patch a tale, oh this fabric's so great!
The seams let out giggles, as we stretch them wide,
In a tapestry woven, with joy as our guide.

So here's to the moments that sparkle and shine,
In this laughter-filled quilt, our dreams intertwine.
Let the mosaic of smiles be the base of our spree,
Where every bright stitch says, "Come laugh here with me!"

The Tangle of Thoughts

In a loo of ideas, I sat quite perplexed,
My brain's got a punchline, but it feels so vexed.
Juggling the phrases like a clown on a ball,
I trip on my tongue, and I'm sure I might fall.

Thoughts dance on page like a bee in a hat,
Spinning and swirling like a dizzying cat.
But when I catch one, it slips from my grip,
And I find myself laughing at this crazy trip.

With a giggle and chuckle, the words take a turn,
Each thought is a flame, watch them twist, spin, and burn.

They twist and they tangle, a hilarious maze,
Where logic has fled, lost in a daze.

So here I embrace all these thoughts that I hold,
Each idea a story, splendid and bold.
In the tangle of thoughts, hilarious and bright,
I find happy laughter, my own personal light.

The Fabric of Feelings

Threading emotions on a quirky old loom,
Tails of delight seem to flourish and bloom.
Each stitch is a chuckle, each knot a delight,
In this fabric of feelings, we wear them so bright.

Laughter is woven with threads of pure cheer,
While sad's in the corner, hiding, I fear.
But bring in the jester with jokes on a roll,
And soon all the stitches will dance to this soul.

Colors of silly are bolder than most,
Woven with giggles, they somehow are toast.
In the fabric of feelings, we play and we spin,
Each emotion a button, let the fun begin!

So let's patch together our quirks and our grins,
With each hearty chuckle, the fun surely wins.
As we wear this creation, let's share every line,
For in laughing together, our hearts intertwine.

Blooms of Belief

In a garden of giggles, ideas take root,
Sprouting up brightly like a dancing grey suit.
Each bloom is a thought, it tickles the mind,
As they twist and they turn, they intertwine.

Watch out for the daisies, the puns are in bloom,
With petals of laughter, they light up the room.
In the petals of dreaming, we toss all our cares,
While the weeds of worry trip over the stairs.

The roses of joy, oh they blossom with cheer,
Their fragrance enchanting, all woes disappear.
As daisies are giggling, and tulips take flight,
In this garden of laughter, we dance into night.

So gather these blooms, make a bouquet of jest,
In the flowers of folly, we find all our best.
With a wink and a smile, our beliefs take a chance,
In the garden of giggles, we happily dance.

Perpetual Patterns

In circles of chuckles, I spin 'round and 'round,
Each loop is a joke, where silliness is found.
Patterns repeating like socks in the wash,
Where laughter's the thread, and I'm quite the posh.

Squares of absurdity, triangles of fun,
I measure my giggles, so none are outdone.
With shiny bright colors, I patch up the seams,
In this quilt of hilarity, I stitch all my dreams.

Though some patterns tangle, don't fret or despair,
For joy's the creation, in chaos we share.
A hat made of whimsy, two pants made of cheer,
The fabric of laughter is ever so near.

So grab all your stiches and thread them today,
In perpetual patterns, let humor lead the way.
With each poke and each prod, there's giggles galore,
In this tapestry woven, who could ask for more?

A Pendant of Phrases

In a tangled vine of chatter,
My tongue trips on every matter.
Words like marbles roll away,
Chasing giggles in the fray.

With phrases dangling in the air,
Like ornaments hung without a care.
Each one slips, then makes a sound,
A chorus of chaos all around.

I wear my jumbles with great pride,
A pendant where my humor hides.
Laughter sparkles like a gem,
At this verbal diadem.

So let's twist and twirl our talk,
And laugh until we cannot walk.
These silly words, a playful spring,
A charm for every silly thing.

Luminescent Lines

In the shimmer of the night,
Words dance in flickering light.
Each sentence glows, a funny sight,
Like fireflies in silly flight.

Rhymes jingle and make us cheer,
A cacophony of good-natured jeer.
As laughter weaves through every phrase,
In this crazy, shining maze.

Witty lines like stars align,
Illuminating wit so fine.
We scribble thoughts on paper bright,
In a whirlwind of pure delight.

So let's gather all our spark,
And play with puns until it's dark.
These luminescent tales we spin,
A joyful glow that lives within.

The Caress of Cadence

In the rhythm of spoken bliss,
Each word a giggle, a playful kiss.
Cadence sways like a fun parade,
Making seriousness quickly fade.

With a hop and a skip, words collide,
Amusing phrases smiling wide.
Like a dance that no one knows,
A frolic that just grows and grows.

The tickle in our throats we share,
Laughter floating in the air.
Each beat a burst of silly fun,
Until we're breathless, everyone.

So take this rhythm, hold it near,
Let it thrum, let it cheer.
For life is but a playful trance,
In every word, a silly dance.

Garden of Linguistic Blooms

In a garden where nonsense grows,
Words bloom bright in funny rows.
With petals like puns so spry,
They make us laugh, oh my, oh my!

Each phrase is planted, nice and neat,
Sprouting giggles, oh, what a treat!
Sunny sentences chase the gloom,
In this riotous linguistic room.

We prune our thoughts for simple cheer,
Watered with laughter, crystal clear.
Every line a flower bold,
In this garden, humor unfolds.

So sniff the blooms, take a stroll,
Let whimsy and jokes take their toll.
For laughter's seeds forever sow,
In this vibrant spot where joy can grow.

Fragrant Lines of Verse

In a garden of phrases, I tripped on a pun,
A daisy of laughter, oh what a fun run!
Each word like a petal, bright colors align,
Tickling the senses, like a grand bottle of wine.

The bees buzz in rhymes, with humor they dance,
Chasing odd metaphors, they frolic and prance.
A sunflower snickers, as shadows grow long,
While the daisies chuckle at a cat's silly song.

But watch out for thorns, wrapped in sarcasm tight,
They poke at your thoughts when you're not in the light.
Yet, in this strange garden, I plant with a grin,
Every joke is a seed, let the laughter begin!

So, gather your verses, let them bloom and blend,
In this merry patch, there's no need to pretend.
With silly wordplay, we'll bloom side by side,
A festival of phrases, where joy is our guide.

Unsung Melodies

Under a tree of alliteration, I whispered a tune,
With squirrels as singers and the sun as my boon.
A chorus of giggles, fluttering about,
Turns simple phrases into party-like shouts.

The frogs found the rhythm, with their croaks in sync,
Jumping to the verses, they never had to think.
A dance on the lily pads, oh what a sight,
Cattails sway to the music, by day and by night.

In puddles of laughter, reflections take shape,
Fish make a splash, in a comical scrape.
Each note is a ripple, tickling the air,
As we waltz through the melodies, without a care.

So play on, dear friends, let your voices be free,
In this jam of a moment, just you and me.
With echoes of humor, let's sing till we fall,
In the symphony of joy, we'll dance through it all.

The Embrace of Eloquence

With eloquent giggles wrapped round my waist,
We twirled through the syllables, a dance most debased.
Language in leggings, a bouncy parade,
Chasing metaphors as they mischievously played.

I tossed around puns like they're candy on streets,
Each line a sweet morsel, that nobody eats.
A chocolate dip phrase makes the critics amused,
While the grammar police look utterly confused.

Such joyous embraces, with each witty jest,
We jive through the chaos, the quirkiest quest.
In the halls of the written, let nonsense unfurl,
As we giggle and bask in this whimsical whirl.

So grab a warm phrase, give it a hug,
Let silliness flourish like a comfortable rug.
In the realm of expression, there's nothing absurd,
For laughter and language are perfectly stirred!

Tapestry of Truths

Woven with thoughts, a tapestry bright,
Threads of banana peels and witty insight.
Each truth is a color, each laugh a fine stitch,
This quirky creation, it's prone to a glitch.

The fabric of folly unfolds in the light,
As snickers spread out, making everything right.
I'll tailor my stories with zany designs,
Where reality dances with cheeky punchlines.

Seams may unravel, but I won't despair,
For sarcasm's thread is woven with care.
In this patchwork of humor, we celebrate glee,
As the fabric of laughter keeps cozy and free.

So gather your chortles, and let them be sewn,
In this whimsical quilt, you're never alone.
With a snip here, a tuck there, it's all a delight,
In the tapestry of truths, let your joy take flight!

Fragments of Expression

A cat with a hat, oh what a sight,
Sipping its tea with all of its might.
The dog looks confused, with eyes so wide,
Wondering if it's time for a ride.

Words tumble out with a shimmy and shake,
Like jelly on toast, what a funny mistake!
"Did I say that?" one would cry with glee,
As they roll on the floor, laughing wildly, you see.

Out comes a frog, with a tad silly grin,
"Hop on!" it shouts, "Let's begin this spin!"
With laughter like bubbles floating around,
They frolic and dance, but fall to the ground.

In this bizarre world where nonsense reigns loud,
The quirks of existence make one very proud.
So join in the fun, don't be shy, my friend,
In fragments we play, let giggles transcend.

Bound by Stanzas

In a world where socks dance, mischief in pairs,
They partner with shoes, in splendid affairs.
With twirls and with jumps, oh what a display,
The mismatched brigade sets the world's heart at bay.

A fish in a bonnet, grinning ear to ear,
Takes to the stage, bringing claps and cheer.
"Is that my lunch?" a seagull seems to think,
But laughter erupts, and they share a wink.

The clouds take a tumble, giggling in flight,
As raindrops of joy sparkle in sunlight.
They playfully rain on the heads of the shy,
While umbrellas bloom, like flowers nearby.

In stanzas we find the peculiar and strange,
Sipping on humor, with just a bit of change.
Bound by the rhythm, let's dance through the night,
In verses of laughter, our hearts take delight.

Ties That Bind

A llama with glasses, looking quite grand,
Sips a smoothie while taking a stand.
"Drink up!" it declares, with a nod and a smile,
As the others just chuckle in a fashionable style.

Words twist like pretzels, all knotted up tight,
They wrestle and tumble, what a curious sight!
"Who let the puns out?" echoes with glee,
As laughter erupts, spreading joy like confetti.

A penguin in pajamas slides down the lane,
"Slippery slope!" it shouts, feeling no pain.
With each little wobble, the giggles ignite,
As friends join the chaos, it's pure dynamite!

With ties that connect us in whims and in fun,
We craft the absurd till the day is done.
So let's raise a toast, and then do a dance,
In this joyful journey, let's take a chance!

A Mosaic of Meaning

A turtle on roller skates zooms past so quick,
Chasing after sunbeams and a candy stick.
It spins and it twirls, in sheer disbelief,
As onlookers burst out in fits of relief.

Words scatter like birds, in fanciful flight,
Flapping and flailing, oh what a sight!
With giggles like sparklers lighting up the air,
They join in a dance without any care.

Jellybeans tumble down from high shelves above,
As grandmothers laugh, caught up in the love.
"Let's have dessert first!" they proclaim with delight,
As the world turns wobbly under bright lights.

This mosaic of moments, so silly and sweet,
Reminds us of laughter in every heartbeat.
So gather your friends, put on that big grin,
And dive into nonsense, where fun will begin!

Gestures in Ink

My pen danced like a chicken,
It scribbled and it clucked.
With every stroke, it was winking,
As my pages became completely plucked.

I inked a cow that wore a hat,
It mooed a tune, quite offbeat.
With laughter, I tried to chat,
But my words tripped over their feet.

The phrases flipped in silly loops,
Like spaghetti on a plate.
They wiggled, jiggled, formed funny groups,
And left my thoughts in a state.

Ink puddles laughed at my mess,
As I tried to find some rhymes.
But each attempt was just excess,
Like jelly on pancakes, it climbs.

The Veil of Silence

Silence wore a funny disguise,
Its veil was made of old shoes.
It tiptoed with great surprise,
Squeaking out a quartet of blues.

While whispers sought a chance to play,
They snickered behind closed doors.
A game of charades on a sunny day,
With gestures that poked at old folklore.

Each hush had a giggle to share,
In corners of the bright café.
And laughter burst forth like a flare,
Over donuts, coffee, and ballet.

But silence, it lost its grand fight,
As humor filled the air's embrace.
Now even mimes took to their flight,
Chatting away with a cheeky grace.

A Tangle of Sentences

Sentences twist like pretzel rods,
Each one trying to break free.
They spiral, twirl, and trip on clods,
Laughing as they bump into me.

Words play chase in a furry race,
Dodging commas, leaping dots.
Syntax struggles with awkward grace,
Tangled tales in goofy knots.

In the corner, adjectives giggle,
Making faces at verbs' mishaps.
Adverbs swirl like a quick little wiggle,
Critiquing each other's silly gaps.

Spellcheck sat with a sigh so deep,
As paragraphs formed a dance floor.
Every error brought laughter, not sleep,
It's a riot, a ruckus, and so much more.

Whispers Among the Leaves

Leaves whispered secrets on the breeze,
Tickling trees with chuckles loud.
Each rustle was a silly tease,
As branches danced, feeling proud.

Among the foliage, jokes took flight,
A leaf cracked up at a twig's jest.
Nature's stand-up made the night,
Giggles echoed from the nest.

Squirrels paused to share a wink,
As acorns dropped with a plop.
Every laugh brought ink to think,
Creating stories that never stop.

In leafy lanes, the humor thrives,
Where every breeze has hearts aglow.
Whispers flourish as joy arrives,
Among the green and all that grow.

www.ingramcontent.com/pod-product-compliance
Lightning Source LLC
Chambersburg PA
CBHW051635160426
43209CB00004B/658